totally fun
beaded
bracelet  guide

Your guide to fun and easy bracelet-making!

by the Spicebox Fun Team

D1451285

This edition published in 2013
By SpiceBox™
12171 Horseshoe Way
Richmond, BC
Canada V7A 4V4

First published in 2007
Copyright © SpiceBox™ 2007

ISBN 10: 1-77132-083-4
ISBN 13: 978-1-77132-083-2

CEO and Publisher: Ben Lotfi
Editorial: Trisha Pope
Creative Director: Garett Chan
Art Director: Christine Covert
Design & Layout: Morgen Price, Mell D'Clute
Production: James Badger, Mell D'Clute
Sourcing: Janny Lam
Photography: James Badger and Garett Chan

Special thanks to the models: Cristina Soares, Renee Lawless,
Jorgina Thompson, Jamie Lacamell, Kelly Chan and Claudia Chan.

For more SpiceBox products and information, visit our website:
www.spiceboxbooks.com

Manufactured in China

1 3 5 7 9 10 8 6 4 2

Table of Contents

Introduction

Making bracelets, rings, earrings and toe rings is simple and fun to do with the fantastic supplies that come in this kit! There really isn't a lot to learn in order to make stylish accessories, and this book will help you with the basics, then give you loads of great ideas and advice for selecting color combinations and patterns.

Use your fashion sense and your imagination and have a great time beading!

Materials

Let's take a look at the contents of your kit.

Beading Tray: This is a handy tool to help you place your beads into the order in which you want to string them, as well as a way to see how many beads you are going to need for your bracelet. We will explain more how to use this tray in the book.

Nylon Stretch Cord: This is what you will string your beads onto for a number of bracelets and rings. It is important to note that sometimes the knots that you tie with this type of cord can slip a bit. For this reason, we recommend that you use a dab of clear nail polish or glue on the knot and let it dry before you wear your bracelet.

Ribbon: We will show you how to make some cute bracelets using ribbon. Ask your parents if they have other bits of ribbon around the house—perhaps from wrapping presents or in their craft supplies.

Beads

There are a few different types of beads in your kit to help you get started with beading.

Seed Beads: These are little doughnut-shaped glass beads. They come in a variety of sizes, and the ones in your kit are "E" beads. These are the largest type of seed bead, and are the easiest to string.

Decorative Beads: There are thousands of types of decorative beads, and although it would be great to put some of everything in the kit, we selected a few different types that work well to mix and match to create the best variety of bracelets. These beads are made out of plastic or acrylic and are easy to use.

Mixed Glass Beads: Although none are included in the kit, a container of mixed glass beads can be purchased in a craft shop very inexpensively. These containers of beads are a fun treasure trove of unique colors and shapes and are a fantastic addition to your beading kit if you wish to expand your supply of beads.

Organizing your beads

If you have ever **tipped over a container of beads,** you will know that those little guys can fly all over the place and take forever to pick up!

It is important to organize your work space. Make sure you have lots of room to work, and that you have larger containers or trays in order to keep the beads you are working with from spilling. While the containers the beads come in are great for storing when you are finished, it is best to have other containers for them while you are working.

Here are some suggestions for good containers you can probably find around the house:

1. Egg cartons. Cut the egg carton into individual sections. Make sure you choose egg cartons that have a flat bottom or they will be tippy!

2. Lids from jars. These work particularly well for the larger beads.

3. Disposable cups. Cut the cups down to about one and a half inches high before you pour your beads into them.

4. Egg cups, saucers, small plastic storage containers, etc. If you ask your parents, they will likely also be able to help you find a variety of small dishes you can use to hold your beads while you work.

Returning your beads to their storage containers:

A great tip for returning unused beads to their little storage container is to pour the beads from the egg carton or cup into a plastic sandwich bag that you snipped the corner off of. Then you can use the bag like a funnel and pour the beads back into the container through the corner of the bag. Be careful to go slowly though or they will bounce out of the container!

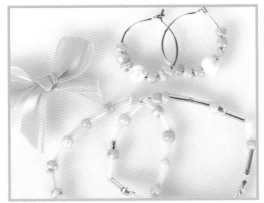

Let's get started!

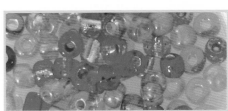

1. To figure out how long to make your bracelet, ask a friend to wrap a piece of nylon cord around your wrist. You want to be sure that it is snug enough that it isn't shifting around a lot, but loose enough that you can get it on and off your wrist. Don't forget, the nylon cord is stretchy, so it should expand over your hand easily.

2. Cut the cord and lay it along the groove in the tray, placing one end at zero and smoothing the length out to see how long it is. This is the length of the finished beaded bracelet.

3. Add four inches to this length so you can tie a knot in it later, and cut a second piece of nylon cord of the final length. For example, if your wrist is four inches around, then add four to this number and cut off an eight-inch length of cord. You can snip off the long ends once the knot is sealed.

4. Choose a color of bead and start to lay them in the groove in the tray, starting at zero. Continue to lay down beads until you have reached the measurement of your wrist, which was the first measurement you took.

5. Wrap a piece of sticky tape on one end of your cord so that the beads don't slide off.

6. Start stringing the beads from your tray onto the longer cord until all of the beads in the tray are on the string.

7. Ask a friend to help you tie your bracelet onto your wrist, making sure to tie a double knot as tightly as possible.

66 This first project is a very simple one to help you use your beading tray and get started making a simple bracelet! 99

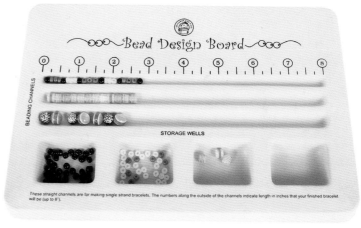

Color coordinating and accessorizing

As we mentioned, beaded bracelets are a great way to accessorize your clothes and create your own fashion style. To help you come up with great color combinations for your bracelets, take a look in your closet, and be inspired by some of your favorite clothes!

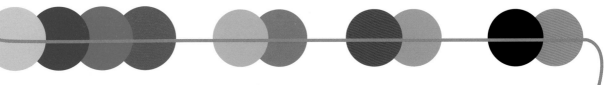

66 Create your own
fashion style **99**

Pick bead colors that
match your clothes:
Corresponding colors are those that will be similar in color to your clothes. It isn't necessary for the colors to match perfectly—in fact, it can look more stylish when they don't—but they should be close in shade to the colors of your outfit.

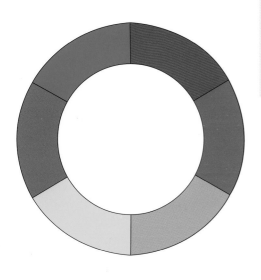

Contrast your clothes:
It can be a lot of fun to wear accessories that "pop" against your clothes, and this normally happens when you pick complementary colors. There are some standard complementary color combinations that are based on the color wheel. Complementary colors normally lie opposite each other on the color wheel.

For example:
With a blue top, wear orange accessories. With purple, wear yellow accessories. With green, wear red accessories.

Some other fun color combinations include black and fuschia, brown and light blue, lime and hot pink.

Take a look at your clothes and see what other fun combinations you can come up with!

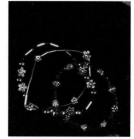

Fantastic jewelry ideas:

Bracelets look particularly fab with jeans and a white t-shirt. With simple clothes like these, your bracelets really stand out. Here are a variety of combinations using blue beads, which will complement your favorite pair of jeans.

Denim blues

Here is a simple repeating pattern. Three blue beads, three white beads, three blue, three white...you get the idea!

The bracelet shown below on the left is similar to the first one, which means they will go well together.

Here is the pattern:

2 x white, 4 x blue, 1 x large iridescent pearl. Repeat this combination until you have the length you need.

Charms: these are a fun addition to bracelets, and we used moon charms because they work well with the blue theme. Scrounge through your jewelry box to see if you have any charms that you can add.

The pattern for the charm bracelet to the right is:
1 x light blue, 2 x blue, 1 x dark blue

Repeat this pattern until you have beaded half of your bracelet. Then, change to this combination:

1 x light blue + charm
2 x blue + charm
2 x blue + charm

2 x blue + charm
2 x blue beads
1 x dark blue bead
and then repeat the pattern until you have your desired length.

Rainbow of

Another way to accessorize jeans and a white t-shirt is by stacking bracelets in bright, contrasting colors.

To make these bracelets, we chose beads that were the same intensity of color, and had the same finish. By doing this, we know that the finished group of bracelets, while being bright and bold against a plain t-shirt, will still all work together and look good stacked on a wrist because they have something in common.

66 This bracelet was easy and fun to make because I chose colors of the rainbow. **99**

This bracelet pattern is:
Blue orange blue, green yellow green. The blue and orange beads really pop out, don't they!

colors

TIP: When using contrasting colors in your accessories, you want the colors to pop out against your clothes, but at the same time you want the bracelets to complement each other. If everything is contrasting, it will look too busy!

The bracelet on the far right was easy and fun to make because I chose colors of the rainbow. The pattern is:
3 × red, 3 × orange, 3 × yellow, 3 × green, 3 × blue. I chose not to add purple because the only bead I had was a light purple. The intensity of the color didn't match the rest of the beads and it looked really strange! Regardless, I think the finished bracelet turned out **very pretty!**

Delightful flowers

This bracelet was a bit trickier to make, but complements the bracelets on the previous pages well. You may want to wear it with fewer bracelets though, so that you can really show it off.

Lay your beads out on your tray in the following order, adjusting the quantity of green beads to fit your wrist.

5 green beads
5 orange beads
5 blue beads
1 large yellow bead for the center of the flower
4 orange beads for the top petals
4 orange beads for the bottom petals
5 blue beads
5 orange beads
5 green beads

Tape the end of your bracelet and start stringing the beads in order until you add the large yellow bead. Once the yellow bead is on, add the first four orange beads.

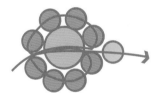

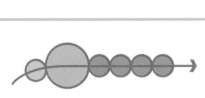

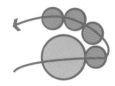

1. Once the orange beads are on the string, take the end of your cord and loop it counterclockwise around the top of the yellow bead.

2. Restring your cord through your yellow bead.

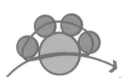

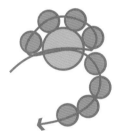

3. Add the next four orange beads and loop them around the bottom of the yellow bead, counterclockwise.

4. Restring your cord through the yellow bead.

5. Add the five blue beads and continue stringing.

Tie around your wrist and add a drop of clear nail polish to the knot.

Going goth

Black, silver and iridescent beads make a wicked combination with black clothes and black nail polish! Experiment with the goth look and play it up when you are heading out shopping or hanging out with friends. Why don't you try a temporary tattoo to add to your edgy look?

66 These bracelets make a **wicked combination** with black clothes and black nail polish. **99**

These bracelets used a lot of the **silver spacer beads interspersed** with **seed beads, bugle beads and iridescent pearls.** The seed beads in these bracelets are smaller than the ones in the kit, and are inexpensive to buy at a dollar store or craft store. They are a bit fussier to string, but give the bracelet a more delicate look.

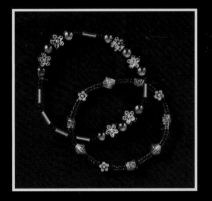

The bugle beads are super easy to string, and because they are long, they make the work of stringing go quite quickly. They look pretty either on their own, or mixed with seed beads or spacer beads. Be careful mixing them with beads that have large holes in them though. Bugle beads are quite thin, so you may find that some beads with large holes will slide right over them!

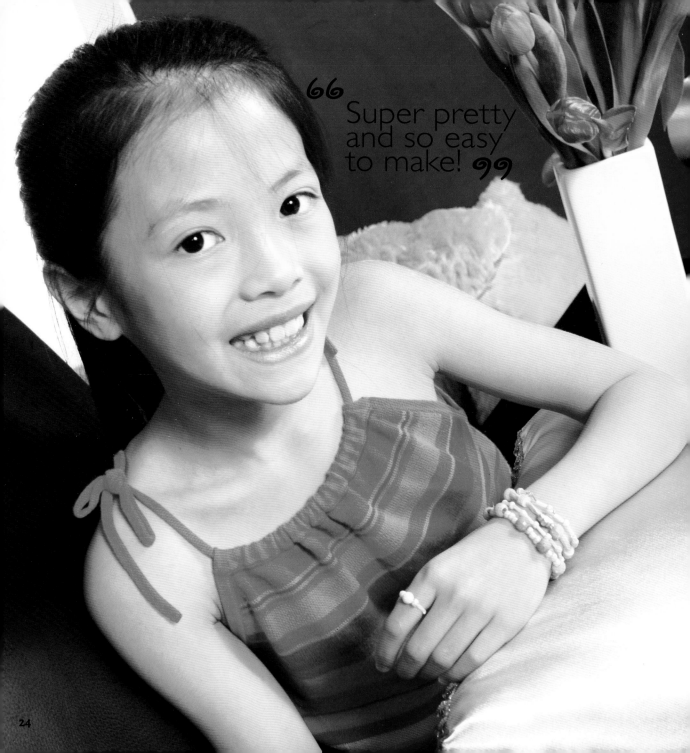

Super pretty and so easy to make!

Charming ribbons

Another fun way to create a bracelet is to use a piece of ribbon and tie it into a bow once you have the beads strung on. It is super easy to do, but there are some tricks that will help you out.

Pick beads with large holes. You probably won't be able to string seed beads or bugle beads onto ribbons very easily, so select some fun, decorative beads with larger holes. Even beads with larger holes will still fit snugly on the ribbon, which makes them easy to space so they won't slide around.

Tie a knot about three inches from one end of the ribbon, and slide your first bead all the way down to the knot, and then space the rest of the beads along the bracelet to the length you want.

Cut the end of the ribbon that you are stringing the beads onto at an angle. The pointy side of the cut will be able to slide through the bead more easily. The end of the ribbon may fray as you are stringing on the beads, so recut the end as you need, in order to make it easier. Once you have all of the beads on the ribbon to the length that fits around your wrist, use a pencil crayon to make a mark on the ribbon beside the last bead. This will mark where you need to tie a knot so the beads don't ever slide off. Push the beads down to the end of the ribbon a bit, so you can knot the ribbon right where the pencil mark is. Then re-space the beads again nicely between the two knots and tie your bracelet onto your wrist!

Tip: You may want to put a bit of fray-stop, which you can get at a fabric store, on the ends of your ribbons to keep them from fraying.

66 Choose
a ribbon that is soft
and is going to
feel comfortable—a
scratchy ribbon
won't be fun to wear! **99**

Mix and Match

with other simple patterns and bracelets.
Ribbon bracelets are pretty and like to
get noticed, so don't try to wear too
many ribbon bracelets at once or your
wrist will start to look crowded! Select
other bracelets that you have made with
coordinating colors of beads but with simple
patterns or styles.

Moon charms

These bracelets are a cheerful combination of gold, clear and yellow beads. I've used seed beads, bugle beads and silver spacer beads as well as charms. A little bit of everything went into this great selection of bracelets! The first step in creating a selection of bracelets that are all different, but work well together, is to select two or three colors you like that you think make a pretty combination. In this group, I selected orange and yellow beads as my main colors, and then picked clear and gold beads as accent colors.

Orange and Silver: (above right)
This bracelet has only one color of glass beads, but I used four different styles of beads. The pattern is: three solid orange seed beads, three clear orange seed beads, one orange bugle bead, one small orange seed bead, one orange bugle bead. Then, I added a silver spacer bead for interest where the pattern ends. Why not try this same pattern in another color?

Orange and Yellow: (far left, and below)

Silver beads add a cool look to your bracelets, but you may not have enough of a single type to use all the way around your bracelet. If this is the case, you can use the silver beads only at the front of the bracelet; this works particularly well to show off an especially pretty one.

The front of the bracelet has a large silver bead in the center, with three smaller ones on each side. The seed beads repeat in a simple pattern around the rest of the bracelet: two yellow, one clear orange, one solid orange. The two orange beads are the same type I used in the orange and silver bracelet previously, so I know that the bracelets will look great together!

Charm Bracelet:

Charms are a fantastic way to express your style and personality! There are so many types of charms available to buy at craft stores that you are sure to find ones that perfectly suit your tastes. It is a good idea when using charms on your bracelet to select other beads that will complement your charms, but not compete with them. In this case, I selected clear beads in yellow and gold so that they go with the other bracelets in the group, but don't look too busy.

Glass beads

I mentioned in the start of the section that a tub of glass beads is an inexpensive and fun way to add to your bead supply. Here you can see some of the fun things that you can do with assorted glass beads if you wish to use them as well.

I had a lot of fun sorting through the beads that I got in my container; you can see from the bracelets I made that they come in all sorts of shapes and sizes, and no two are really the same!

Start by picking out a few that you really like, and then see if you can find others that are a similar shape or color. Make little groups of glass beads that you like, and then pick a seed bead or other type of bead that you can combine them with to create a pretty look. **You may also want to try threading them onto ribbon.**

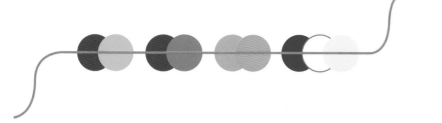

Here are some great combinations that you may want to try:

Combine brown glass beads with yellow seed beads for a sophisticated style that will look good with practically anything you wear.

I also love turquoise and brown together, and thought they looked sharp with clear seed beads. Very chic!

Put on pretty frosted pink nail polish to create a fabulous look with a bracelet made with green glass beads and pink seed beads.

Combine blue glass beads with blue or white seed beads for a bracelet that will look great with your jeans.

Easy earrings

66 Be creative
and have fun! 99

Hoop earrings are simple and fun to make. Just like making bracelets, it is really just a matter of selecting your favorite beads and sliding them onto the wires. Make sure you leave room for them to fit onto your ears and still close.

These pretty pink little hoops were a cinch to make. With three pink seed beads, one pearl and three more seed beads, you will be able to wear these hoops with lots of different outfits! They will go beautifully with the pink beaded bracelets we made to match.

Here are other cool looks to try.

32

Bright and cheerful

By now you should be very comfortable creating fabulous new bracelets, but just in case you need a few more ideas, here are some more simple patterns you can try, this time using decorative beads.

2 x green "E" beads
2 x frosted green small seed beads
2 x green "E" beads
1 x decorative bead

With this bracelet, I alternated between a yellow decorative bead and an orange one in the same style. With the next bracelet, I again used the same style of decorative bead, but this time alternating orange with blue. The pattern is quite easy, and the bracelet looks great with the one shown on page 18.

2 x yellow beads
2 x blue beads
1 x decorative orange bead
2 x blue beads
2 x yellow beads
1 x decorative blue bead

Blue flowers

Mixing and matching beads is a lot of fun. Although your kit has plenty to choose from, there are lots of other fun beads available to use. I really like working with bugle beads—the skinny tube beads—as well as smaller sizes of seed beads. Here are some bracelets using a variety of beads.

Bugles and Flowers
The holes in decorative beads can sometimes be quite large. In this case, the flower beads slid right over the bugle beads on the bracelet! In order to keep all the beads in their proper place, I strung a seed bead on each side of the flower beads. It helps to keep the flower beads from sliding around on the bracelet, and it looks pretty!

Daisy Bracelet
This pretty bracelet combines decorative beads with seed beads. It is a charming bracelet that looks great with anything you put on!

Small Seed Beads

Small seed beads create a totally different look to your bracelet. They are harder to string, and, unless you have a super skinny beading needle to use, I recommend you only try to string them onto the stiffer nylon strings. However, they do create a lovely look to your bracelets. They are more delicate-looking and create a thinner bracelet, and they mix well with the larger seed beads in your kit. Here I found a color that went well with the decorative flower bead in the center, and strung the whole bracelet with that color. Quite charming!

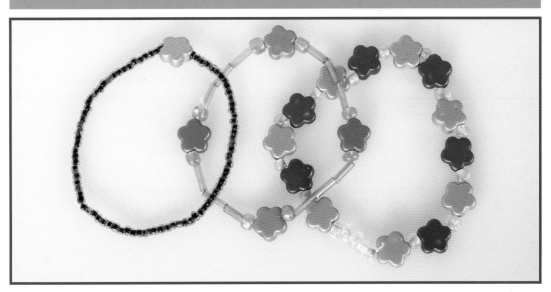

Double strands of pink

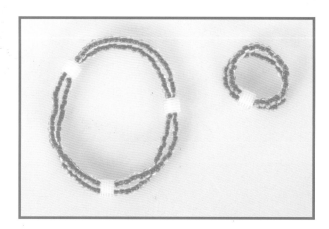

As you have seen, making bracelets can be as easy as stringing your favorite beads onto your string, knotting it and slipping your new accessory on your wrist. However, there are tons of other things you can do with beads to make stylish and fun jewelry. Here is an idea that works just as well with beaded rings as it does with bracelets.

To make the bracelet, cut a length of cord twice as long as you normally would to make a single-strand bracelet. Count out twice as many seed beads as well, and three decorative beads.

Lay one decorative bead at the start of the row on your beading tray. Add half of the seed beads that you selected and set the other half aside for the moment. Finally, insert a second decorative bead one third of the way down the row, and the final one two thirds down the row of seed beads.

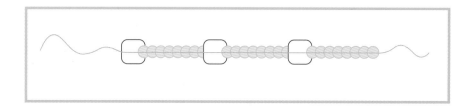

1. Tape your string to your work surface—leaving about two inches at the top for knotting. String the beads from the tray onto your string.

2. Now, pull the end of your string around to the decorative bead that you strung first. Push your string through this bead again and pull tight to close the bracelet.

3. Start stringing the remaining seed beads you selected initially until you reach the second decorative bead.

4. Push your string through the second decorative bead and continue adding seed beads until you reach the third decorative bead. String through this bead and add the rest of your seed beads.

5. Carefully untape your bracelet and tie the loose ends together. Add a drop of clear polish so your bracelet doesn't come undone.

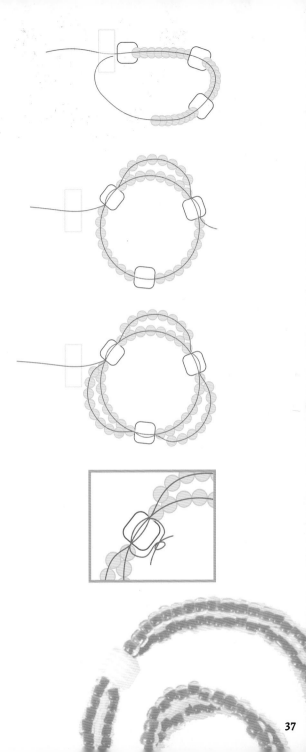

Lovely rose

With shades of dark pink and rose, larger burgundy glass beads, silver spacers and charms, these bracelets are lovely and can be worn with everything from jeans and a t-shirt, to a pretty summer dress. The bracelet above on the right is a variation of the double-strand bracelet made on page 36.

The bracelet on the left has a simple pattern of two light pink beads alternating with two dark rose beads. A cross charm was added in the center of the bracelet with two silver decorative beads on either side. Of course, any type of charm would work equally well, so make your own look with your favorite charms.

In the bracelet below the same charm was used with silver spacer beads on each side, but the look is totally different because only dark rose seed beads were used, interspersed with cool, unmatched glass beads. The glass beads are all different, but because they are roughly the same shape and color, they work well together.

Follow the steps on page 36 to make the double-strand bracelet pictured on page 38. Instead of using a single color of seed beads though, I used both the light pink and dark rose colors that are in the other bracelets. They were laid out randomly though, in no particular order. Then, instead of the three matching decorative beads, six glass beads in assorted shapes were inserted. Even though they are all different sizes and colors, they are all in the same family of colors as the seed beads. Overall, the effect is lovely, and looks far more complicated than it is!

66...looks far more complicated
than it is!**99**

Word play

Express yourself by stringing words, phrases or a name together with delightful brights or pastel-colored beads like these—be creative!

You now have lots of hints, tips and ideas to help you create your own wonderful jewelry. We hope you enjoy making, wearing and sharing your designs.

Happy beading!